HOMEOPATHIC REMEDIES FOR CHILDREN'S COMMON AILMENTS

SAFE, EFFECTIVE, DRUGLESS TREATMENTS FOR EVERYDAY HEALTH PROBLEMS

Carolyn Dean, M.D.

Keats Publishing, Inc.   New Canaan, Connecticut

ABOUT THE AUTHOR

Carolyn Dean received her M.D. from Dalhousie University in Halifax, Nova Scotia, Canada. She had a private practice in nutritional medicine in Toronto for 12 years, incorporating herbs, homeopathy, acupuncture and nutrition. Dr. Dean now lives in New York where she does clinical research in homeopathic acupuncture. She is the author of the highly acclaimed *Complementary Natural Prescriptions for Common Ailments* published by Keats Publishing, Inc.

HOMEOPATHIC REMEDIES FOR CHILDREN'S COMMON AILMENTS

ISBN: 0-87983-668-7

Printed in the United States of America

Good Health Guides are published by
Keats Publishing, Inc.
27 Pine Street (Box 876)
New Canaan, Connecticut 06840-0876

INTRODUCTION

Homeopathy is the safest, least expensive and quickest acting method of treating children for common ailments. It is also the fastest growing over-the-counter therapy for common children's ailments. Most health food stores and many pharmacies are now carrying homeopathic remedies. If you have your own kit of commonly prescribed remedies it is wonderful to have something at hand in the middle of the night to start treating your child immediately. Then you have a chance to make an assessment of the severity of the condition and see whether or not to take your child to the doctor. There is a concern among some practitioners that parents should not treat their children but rather bring every inquiry to the doctor. This is for you, the parent, to decide. You know your child better than anyone and instinctively and intuitively can often tell when something is serious and when it is not. Of course, when it is serious or when in doubt, be sure to seek medical help.

Homeopathic remedies come in tiny pellet form or in liquid form. The pellets are made from milk sugar; however milk sensitive people do not usually display an allergic reaction to this tiny amount. However if your child is allergic to milk, check with your doctor first before using pellets and perhaps just order the liquid form. Be careful to keep the dropper clean and sterile. Do not put the dropper right into the child's mouth and risk getting germs on it. Some parents put the drops of remedy in water and give the water to the child or put the drops on a teaspoon and feed this to the child.

Children find this form of therapy quite acceptable and pleasant; even so, make sure they realize it is medicine and not candy. Homeopathic remedies cannot be overdosed and cannot be toxic like pharmaceutical drugs, but it is wise to keep them out of the reach of children.

HOW TO USE HOMEOPATHIC REMEDIES

DOSAGE ADVICE

The potency for each of these remedies, for most of the conditions listed, is 6c or 30c. Four drops is the usual dosage amount if the remedy is in liquid form; if the remedy is in white pellet form, use two to four pellets per dose.

The frequency of dosage depends on the acuteness or chronicity of the condition. For acute conditions the drops are given every few minutes combined with lots of reassurance. If the symptoms do not abate after two or three doses, choose another remedy.

As the symptoms lessen give four drops every 30 to 60 minutes. Then go to four drops three times per day.

If, after trying two or three remedies over a period of several hours with no change in symptoms, be sure to consult a medical doctor.

For mild conditions that are not serious, if one remedy doesn't work within one or two days, another remedy should be tried. If several fail to have effect, a homeopathic doctor should be consulted for more specific advice.

REMEMBER: WHEN IN DOUBT ABOUT ANY SYMPTOM, CONSULT A MEDICAL DOCTOR.

CARE AND USAGE

1. Do not expose to radiation such as the X-ray machines at the airport. Carry your remedies in a double-lead film shield bag to prevent exposure at high altitudes by high altitude radiation. Keep away from computers. Keep out of direct sunlight.

2. Keep away from strong smelling household products, aromatherapy and heavy scents.

3. Do not consume caffeine, chamomile or mint products as these can neutralize homeopathic remedies.

ADENOIDS

• **Barium carb** is used for children who are underdeveloped physically and mentally.

• **Calc carb** is for pasty, puffy, chilly, clammy children who have head sweats at night.

• **Calc phos** is for thin children with large adenoids out of proportion to their size.

• **Psorinum** is for children who along with their enlarged adenoids have itchy skin and offensive, toxic, acrid sweat.

• **Sulphur** is for children who are ravenous at mid-morning, who don't like showers or baths and who have large obstructing adenoids.

ALLERGIES

Spring hay fever can be treated with preventive homeopathic combination remedies. Before spring, oral doses of homeopathic *Grasses, Pollens and Trees* can be taken.

In the fall, ragweed allergies can be avoided by taking homeopathic *Ragweed* or *Ambrosia* as well as *Mold*. The rain and dampness in the fall as the leaves fall and go moldy cause a lot of symptoms that can be avoided. The remedies can be continued as long as symptoms persist.

Homeopathic remedies for hay fever symptoms:

• **Allium cepa** is used for episodes of sneezing with burning in the nose and excoriation of the upper lip from watery and profuse discharge. The symptoms are better with cold compresses on the face.

• **Arsenicum** is for sneezing and nasal burning but symptoms are better with hot water on the face in the form of compresses.

• **Calc carb** is for a pale, overweight child with head sweats.

- **Euphrasia** is for a child with mostly eye symptoms of burning and watery eye discharge. The nasal discharge does not burn.

- **Hydrastis** is for allergies with a thick yellow-green discharge. There are usually crusts of mucus in the nose.

- **Natrum mur** is specific for cracked dry lips, upper lip infections and painful nasal boils.

- **Pulsatilla** is for nasal stuffiness that is worse indoors and at night. Symptoms are much less outdoors in cool air.

Homeopathic remedies for various food allergies also exist. For example there is a *Wheat* remedy. This could be used for a child with a wheat allergy to desensitize him or her to wheat. However at the same time wheat should be avoided or consumed only every fourth day. One must be very careful with allergies to foods, particularly peanuts, which can cause anaphylaxis. Presumably no simple form of desensitization will take away severe allergic reactions. Avoidance is the only safe approach in these cases.

ANEMIA

Babies who have been breast fed may have a tendency to anemia from insufficient iron. If this is the case, homeopathic remedies can help.

- **Ferrum met** is homeopathic iron and can help the body's absorption and utilization of iron.

- **Calc carb** can be used especially in young girls who have been anemic since infancy. There is a tendency to gain weight. There is much mucus and diarrhea. The child is weak and complains of palpitations and dizziness on exertion.

ANOREXIA NERVOSA

This condition mostly affects girls when they are beginning to experience the sometimes chaotic changes associated with puberty and adolescence. Some say controlling eating is their way of staying in control and not having to grow up.

In its mild, acute or beginning stage it may appear as a

short-term loss of appetite which if treated promptly will resolve and not develop into the syndrome.

• **Aconite** is for children who have no appetite because they are afraid.

• **Arsenicum** is also for fear of eating but due to fear of being poisoned. The child is also restless and becomes exhausted with the tension. There may also be vomiting.

• **Gelsemium** is for the apathetic, weak, withdrawn child who wants to be given a reason why she should eat. There is also insomnia and lack of thirst.

• **Ignatia** is for the histrionic child who equates eating with getting fat and simply refuses to eat to live. This child feels rejected and is obsessed with attaining the perfect weight. She may also have physical complaints such as severe headaches.

• **Natrum mur** is for the more depressed child who fears rejection, appears very dry and dehydrated with dry lips and skin and constipation.

• **Phosphoric acid** is for the child who rejects food due to grief and becomes apathetic.

ANAL FISSURE

• **Aesculus** is for burning tenderness and low back pain.

• **Graphites** is for pain and soreness of the anus.

• **Nitric acid** is for sharp cutting pain.

• **Ratanhia** is for burning after a bowel movement with knife-like pain.

• **Silicea** is for slow healing anal fissures.

• **Tuberculinum** is for fissures with rectal fullness and diarrhea.

APPETITE LOSS

• **Calc carb** is for aversion to meat.

• **Ignatia** is for loss of appetite for all food.

• **Nux vomica** is for a bitter taste in the mouth; the tongue has a thick yellow coating.

• **Lycopodium** is given for a full feeling after only a few bites of food.

• **Pulsatilla** is for the child who has no desire for liquids as well as no appetite.

• **Rhus tox** is for an aversion to all food.

ASTHMA

This condition occurs when the bronchial tubes and the smaller airways in the lungs tighten up and cause shortness of breath and wheezing. In children, the condition can be due to allergies, a pre-existing bronchial infection or stress. If the stress is physical exertion, the condition is called exercise-induced asthma.

Diet is extremely important. Have your child checked for food as well as inhalant allergies including dust, animal danders and smoke. Also, avoid smoke-filled environments, incense, cigarettes or wood burning fires. Use air conditioners and air cleaners.

In an acute attack try to give lots of fluids so the lungs don't get dry and turn the mucus into dry plugs that block the breathing even more. Make sure your child is urinating. If only tiny amounts of urine are produced, it means she is dehydrated.

Homeopathic remedies for asthma include:

• **Aconite** is for asthma with sudden onset, especially that brought on by exposure to cold. There is also great fear expressed with this type.

• **Antimonium tart** is for loud, heavy wheezing.

• **Arsenicum** is especially for night asthma with panics. The fear and restlessness, of course, only make the breathing worse. As with all acute symptoms, if the attack does not subside, medical assistance should be sought.

• **Ipecacuanha** is for symptoms of a blocked nose and heavy mucus in the throat but little sputum production.

• **Veretrum viride** is for asthma with cold sweats and nausea and vomiting. These are symptoms of shock.

BED WETTING

The causes for bedwetting are often related to psychological stress, especially if a sibling is born around the time when the older child has been dry at night for several months. The bedwetting can be an attention-getting device on an unconscious psychological level. Other stresses in the home can result in bedwetting. Sleep-overs often produce bedwetters because of the excitement and stress of sleeping away from home.

However, also look for food allergies that can contribute to irritation or relaxation of the bladder neck muscles which allow the urine to leak during the night. The urination can come during the very deep sleep phase when there is not enough arousal to wake a child up and allow him to go to the bathroom.

The foods that seem to cause the most problems are milk, orange juice, peanut butter and sugar, but almost any food could conceivably cause the problem. Drinking before bed itself can fill the bladder and lead to bedwetting. Limiting food intake after supper would be appropriate. Also, getting the child up to urinate when the adults are going to bed would help to keep the bladder empty.

The homeopathic remedies for bedwetting include:

• **Arsenicum** is for children who are nervous, restless, toss and turn, have lots of fear. The bedwetting tends to occur when the child is left alone or is feeling insecure.

• **Benzoic acid** is for children with strong-smelling urine; the odor fills the whole room. The urine can cause stains in the sheets that can't be washed out.

• **Causticum** is for children who wet immediately on going to bed.

• **Cina** is used in cases of urethral or bladder irritation. The irritation itself may be coming from the colon and may be due to pinworms. These children grind their teeth, are irritable and have ravenous appetites.

• **Equisetum** is for children with profuse, watery, pale urine.

• **Lycopodium** is for children who wet the bed and may also dribble all day. They express fear and insecurity or fright, often from harsh parents or siblings. They hold in their urine all day and at night go to sleep and relax and the floodgates are opened. Then they get punished or teased and get even more tense the next day.

• **Natrum mur** is for children who try to hide their bedwetting. They feel they are not getting enough love and affection. They may be so controlled that they won't urinate outside the home.

• **Phosphorus** is for bedwetting due to drinking at night. It helps to stop giving the child water at night as well as to use this remedy.

• **Pulsatilla** is for bladder weakness and dribbling. This problem is found in children who are soft and sensitive, weepy and changeable.

• **Sepia** is for bedwetting in the first hour, as soon as the body is relaxed. There is weakness of the bladder and a cough or sneeze will cause a leak.

• **Thuja** is for multiple floods every night, as many as five or six times per night. The child may even wake up with the urge but can't get to the bathroom.

BITES
The homeopathic remedies for bites and stings include:

• **Apis,** which itself is made from bee-sting venom.

When a child has a bee-sting allergy, the remedy can be

used every few minutes; however, one should always carry an Anakit (bee-sting kit) which contains adrenaline, a syringe and a needle to be used especially if the sting is around the face or throat.

• **Ledum** is a remedy for tick bites, spider bites or even cat and dog bites. These bites can produce an infection, and the area should be cleaned well and should be examined by a doctor, who may advise an antibiotic cream, a tetanus booster or possibly antibiotics by mouth.

BLADDER INFECTION
In young girls, bladder infections can be the result of taking bubble baths, and of course this should be avoided in sensitive children.

• **Apis** is a remedy for severe cystitis with edema of the urethra. The child is not thirsty and screams out in pain.

• **Benzoic acid** is used for offensive urine which is dark and smells of ammonia.

• **Berberis** is for cystitis with left-sided back pain coming from kidney involvement.

• **Cantharis** is used for knifelike pain during urination with severe burning and cutting pain and spasms. Small amounts are passed and there may be blood in the urine.

• **Causticum** is used for burning pain during urination. There may be chronic incontinence and dribbling which is worse with coughing, sneezing or laughing. The urine is frequent and scanty.

• **Equisetum** is for cystitis with copious amounts of pale urine, urinary frequency, but no relief from urination.

• **Lycopodium** is for cystitis with right-sided kidney pain, urgency and frequency. The child is better with hot drinks.

• **Phosphorus** is for urgency, frequency and blood in the urine.

• **Pulsatilla** is for children with cystitis who are helpless, crying, pitying themselves and thirstless. They experience incontinence but the cystitis is not severe.

• **Sarsaparilla** is for right-sided kidney pain with burning at the end of urination of frequent small amounts.

• **Staphasagria** is for burning pain during or between urinations. This problem is usually due to tissue irritation, which in children can be due to bubble baths or after catheterization.

BOILS
Homeopathic treatments include oral doses of:

• **Apis** for the redness and swelling around the boil.

• **Arnica** for boils with bruising pain from being in sensitive areas.

• **Arsenicum** for boils with burning pain.

• **Hepar sulph** to bring boils to a head.

• **Mercurius sol** for boils in the ears.

• **Calc sulph** for recurring crops of boils.

• **Silicea** for boils that are slow to develop and slow to heal.

• **Sulphur** for burning and itching boils that spread and worsen because the child can't stop scratching.

An herbal tincture of *echinacea* can be used, ten to 15 drops three times a day in four ounces of water, to soak a boil. Other boil soaks are *hypericum* tincture and *calendula* tincture.

BRONCHITIS
There are many homeopathic remedies for bronchitis.

• **Aconite** is used for its keynote, sudden onset. Therefore it is used in the early stages.

• **Antimonium tart** is used when there is loud rattling of mucus in the lungs.

- **Arsenicum** is for the child who has lots of coughing but little sputum and is worse at night.

- **Bryonia** is for a dry hacking cough with pain in the chest.

- **Hepar sulph** is for a wet cough and profuse yellow sputum.

- **Ipecacuanha** is for a cough which leads to gagging and vomiting.

- **Kali bich** is for tenacious sticky mucus that is hard to bring up.

- **Pulsatilla** is for weepy children who are worse lying down and worse in a warm room.

- **Sulphur** is for the later or chronic stages where the cough is worse in bed at night and the child has dry skin and is irritable.

BRUISING

For bruises caused by an injury, the most important treatment is *arnica* 30c or 200c by mouth, and arnica cream on the bruise as long as the bruise does not break the skin. Arnica is a mountain plant that is quite amazing for anything from a black eye to a stubbed toe. The more serious the injury, the more frequently the arnica is taken, anywhere from every 15 minutes to every two hours. Ice is also useful for the first 24 or 36 hours to stop the inflammation. The ice packs should be applied every 15 to 20 minutes. After 36 hours, heat can be used to clear the dead blood cells from the area by increasing the circulation.

- **Hypericum** is for bruising of toes, fingers or tailbone, which are rich in nerve endings, causing severe pain.

- **Ruta grav** is for bruising of bones and tendons.

BULIMIA

- **Aurum met** is for a child who is depressed or melancholy. There is a tendency to self-destruct which may manifest as bulimia. Even though there may be good appetite, the child can't take in the food and she gags and vomits.

• **Kali phos** is another remedy for depression. The child feels a hollowness in the stomach and vomits easily after eating.

• **Lycopodium** treats melancholy and loneliness. This child has an insatiable appetite but only eats a few mouthfuls and feels bloating and indigestion. There is much flatulence and burping and cycles of vomiting begin in an effort to feel more comfortable.

• **Natrum carb** is for a child who gets tired easily both mentally and physically. The digestion is weak and ravenous hunger gives way to bloating, nausea and vomiting with a heaviness in the stomach.

• **Phosphorus** is for the child who feels emptiness in the stomach and spaciness in the head. There are cravings for bubbly drinks and sweets. There is hunger immediately after eating and much embarrassment.

• **Pulsatilla** is for the child who is lonely and depressed. There is an obsession around weight and the whole attitude and behavior revolves around appetite and eating.

BURNS

The immediate treatment for burns is cold water on the burn and oral ingestion of an homeopathic remedy.

•**Cantharis** can be taken every few minutes by mouth. *Cantharis* liquid tincture, diluted and applied directly to the burn, is also extrtemely helpful. This should be in everyone's first aid kit. You must never break a burn blister because this can allow infection. The burn blister protects the underlying skin while it heals.

•**Causticum** is for painful burn scars and to prevent scarring.

•**Hepar sulph** is for burns that have not been kept clean and have become infected.

• **Kali bich** is for serious second degree burns.

• **Urtica urens** is for stinging pain of a burn, either early on or as the skin is healing and stretching.

CANKER SORES

A canker sore can be one or more ulcerations on the mucous membrane of the mouth. The most common cause of canker sores in the mouth is too many acidic foods in the diet. In children this would include citrus fruits, tomatoes, chewable vitamin C and chocolate. A mechanical imbalance of the biting surface of the teeth can lead to accidental biting at the sides of the inner cheek and cause trauma that will lead to cankers. Also, improper use of a toothbrush by a child can cause scrapes and damage. Food allergies and candidiasis can also cause cankers.

The treatment for cankers is to avoid acidic foods and use acidophilus or yogurt to restore normal bacterial flora in the mouth.

• **Borax** is used for canker sores on the tongue and the insides of the cheeks. The child is very restless, even nervous and sensitive to noise. The mouth appears hot and the lesions are very painful.

• **Baptisia** is given for small painful ulcers which prevent the child from eating food. The child only takes fluids and the breath is very offensive.

• **Mag carb** is for chronic canker sores in a child who is weak, allergic and hypersensitive.

CAVITIES

Cavities often plague young children who are given bottles of juice at bedtime. Bacteria feeding on the extremely high fructose content drill holes in the teeth. Never use anything but water in a bottle if it is being used as a soother.

• **Cal carb** can be used to help strengthen the teeth and prevent decay in a fat, flabby child with late eruption of teeth and early signs of decay.

CHICKENPOX

Chickenpox is a virus characterized by a rash with fluid-filled eruptions surrounded by a red halo. The rash occurs first on the trunk of the body and later spreads to the face, arms and legs. With extensive and severe cases the rash can spread to the palms and soles and to the mucous membranes of the mouth. After contact the incubation time is between 12 and 21 days. The disease begins with a headache, a fever and fatigue.

• **Aconite** is the first remedy to consider in the early stages of all viral illnesses including chickenpox. There will be a fever but no sweating and the child will be fearful, anxious and thirsty.

• **Belladonna** is used in chickenpox where there is fever, sore throat and a skin flush that leaves a pale circle around the lips. There is also a severe throbbing headache.

• **Pulsatilla** is for children who are soft, tearful and thirstless.

• **Antimonium tart** suits children who demand constant attention and are also irritable.

• **Sulphur** is for a hot child who is very thirsty and drinks a lot but has no appetite.

• **Rhus tox** is used when the blisters first form and is said to be the most often used and best remedy for chickenpox.

CHRONIC FATIGUE SYDROME

This illness is a collection of signs and symptoms that appear to be related to the overactivity of the immune system as it tries to cope with numerous low grade infections. Children can experience chronic weakness, sore throat, muscle aches and pains, headaches, inability to concentrate and sleep problems.

Since this condition affects the whole body, it is best to work with a homeopathic physician to determine the constitutional remedy that best suits your child.

• **Ignatia** is for the sensitive and even hysterical child who cannot believe that the world would be so cruel as to make him sick.

• **Natrum mur** is for the hypochondriacal child who may be very ill this time but is hard to believe for having cried wolf too often. She is very sad and weepy and demands comfort but when it is offered she gets offended.

• **Nux vomica** is for the child who works and plays too hard and can collapse as a result.

Colds and Flus
The most common remedies are:

• **Aconite** can be used for the first signs of a cold or flu. Usually the symptoms begin after exposure to cold air and the child is visibly chilled. The symptoms are worse after midnight but better with fresh air. The child is also anxious and thirsty.

• **Allium cepa** is used in cases where the eyes and the nose are running and the discharge is burning and causes a lot of sneezing.

• **Arsenicum** is for flu symptoms with tossing and turning, anxiety, restlessness and thirst.

• **Belladonna** is an acute remedy for symptoms which explode within hours with headache, sore throat, earache, swollen tonsils, swollen glands and a high fever. The face may flush quickly and be very hot with dilated pupils.

• **Bryonia** is for flu symptoms with tension and irritability, worse with movement; the child wants to be left alone. There is a headache with sharp pain, dry mouth and thirst.

• **China** is for recurrent flu.

• **Eupatorium perf** is for colds and flus that affect the bones with deep pain; the chest is very sore. The child is also thirsty and has a cough. Symptoms are worse with cold air. This is the remedy for 'break-bone fever.'

• **Gelsemium** is for colds and flus due to overwork and

exhaustion with slow onset and vague muscle aches, heavy legs, a band-like headache and chills running up and down the spine. There is a fever but the child is not thirsty. This type of flu can come from stage fright or the effects of anticipation which leaves the child drained and vulnerable.

• **Dulcamara** is for colds and flus developing at the end of summer and into fall.

• **Natrum mur** is used for symptoms of a thin, watery but profuse nasal discharge. The child may be sneezing and have lost the sense of smell and taste.

• **Nux vomica** is for children with nasal congestion which is worse at night but becomes runny during the day. The discharge may be burning and the child is very irritable and impatient.

• **Ferrum phos** is for the beginning of a cold.

• **Hepar sulph** is used for a left-sided sore throat with a cold.

• **Kali bich** is for colds and sinusitis with tough stringy mucus.

• **Pulsatilla** is for a cold with thick yellow mucus.

• **Rhus tox** is for symptoms of a flu with stiffness and restlessness which may occur after heavy exertion or exercise. The symptoms occur or are worse in cold weather.

COLD SORES/HERPES SIMPLEX

This is a recurrent viral infection mostly on or around the lips. Tiny blisters or vesicles filled with slightly yellowish fluid appear after a day of nerve tingling at the site. The first time herpes appears, however, it can be a full-blown viral infection with fever, muscle aches, lack of appetite, and swollen neck glands as well as cold sores in and around the mouth and even into the throat. In infants and children great care must be taken to keep the infection from being spread to the eyes. This would constitute a medical emergency.

• **Arsenicum** treats the burning shooting pain of cold sores which are worse at night. These lesions are large and deep with thick crusts that bleed when taken off.

- **Borax** is specific for children's cold sores with white ulcerated edges that then crust over.

- **Calc carb** suits children who are chubby, chilly and cheerless. The lesions ulcerate and are very painful.

- **Dulcamara** is used for cold sores that come with change of season to cold and wet, such as in the fall. The lesions are likewise moist and hold a lot of fluid.

- **Natrum mur** is used for the first outbreak of herpes with a fever and dry cracked lips. There is pain and itching and a clear watery fluid in the vesicles.

- **Rhus tox** treats cold sores that resemble poison ivy with severe burning and itching.

- **Silicea** is for recurrent cold sores that fail to heal.

Colic

For colic in breast-fed babies, especially if your baby burped or hiccoughed in the womb, watch what you eat. The baby may be reacting to something that doesn't agree with her in your diet. Cut out strong tasting foods first; then cut out dairy and wheat.

This is a condition of smooth muscle spasm and excess gas in the intestinal tract of infants. During a colic attack, carry the infant face down along your forearm with its head in your hand and its legs astride your elbow. This puts comforting pressure on its rumbling abdomen. Colic is also related to the stress and anxiety of the parents. The child picks up on their nervousness immediately so parents under stress should seek help.

The homeopathic remedies are:

- **Aethusa** for colic from sensitivity to breast milk.

- **Pulsatilla** is for gentle, usually happy babies who need to be held, rocked and moved all the time.

- **Chamomilla** is for whiny, irritated and irritating babies who seem as frustrated as you feel.

- **Cina** is for colic with lots of gas, with or without pinworms.

- **Mag carb** and **mag phos** is for colic which seems to be better with heat and pressure.

If symptoms persist, seek the advice of a doctor or pediatrician to make sure there is nothing more serious going on.

COLITIS
Colitis is a condition of bowel diarrhea and inflammation. The causes in natural medicine are attributed to improper food digestion. This could mean food sensitivities, allergies or a less than perfect diet which can cause bowel irritation. The most common cause is excess wheat or dairy in a person who is unable to digest these foods.

- **Argentum nit** is for worsening from excitement or anticipation of an event.
- **Arsenicum** is for colitis that is worse after midnight.
- **Colchicum** is for profuse watery stools.
- **Colocynthis** is for colitis with severe colic.

CONCUSSION
This is a medical emergency in a child, but once the child has been released from the hospital, homeopathy can be used. However if symptoms persist, return to the hospital for observation.

- **Arnica** is used when there is bruising from the injury.
- **Helleborus** is used for residual headache and lethargy.
- **Hypericum** is for a persistent sharp pain in the head.
- **Natrum mur** is for depression following the head injury.

CONJUNCTIVITIS or Pink Eye
- **Aconite** is used during the early stages with redness of the white part of the eye.
- **Argentum nit** is for a yellow discharge from the eye.
- **Arsenicum** is for burning, watery eye discharge.

• **Euphrasia** is for the child who has lots of watery discharge which burns; the eyelids are also irritated and sore.

CONSTIPATION

Constipation is often observed in infants when switching from breast to bottle or when introducing solids. The bottle formula may be too high in solutes and may need to be diluted. Or, it may also be a reaction to processed dairy or wheat; try avoiding these foods for a period of two to three weeks to see if it makes a difference. Also, increase diluted fruit juices and water. Stress and tension in or between the parents can translate into a holding back by the child which can manifest as constipation.

There are many homeopathic remedies for constipation. These can be used for a short term to stimulate the body's own vital force to change this condition.

• **Nux vomica.** A constant ineffectual urge to have a bowel movement is present in those who need this remedy. It is also used when the stool does occur but is incomplete and unsatisfactory as though some were left behind. Nux vomica is also useful to antidote purgative medicines that have long been used to treat constipation.

• **Sulphur** can be used alternating with nux vomica. Sulphur treats ineffectual urging to stool with a sensation of heat and discomfort in the rectum and an uneasy feeling all through the intestinal tract due to gas and bloating. The stools are hard, dry, dark and expelled with great straining and often with great pain. There may also be constipation alternating with diarrhea.

• **Alumina** is used for very hard dry stools which may cause bleeding.

• **Bryonia** is for hard, dry but very bulky stools even though the child drinks plenty of liquids.

• **Lycopodium** is for constipation where there is much intestinal movement of gas but no bowel movements.

• **Nitric acid** is for painful bowel movements as from sharp sticks with bleeding.

CONVULSIONS

This is another medical emergency that requires a doctor's attention. However, after diagnosis the following remedies can be considered to treat aftereffects.

• **Aconite** is for convulsions caused by fright or fever.

• **Belladonna** is for convulsions from a high fever where the child is flushed and the pupils are dilated and the child may be hallucinating.

• **Cuprum met** is for convulsions brought on by paroxysms of whooping cough; the fingers and toes are in spasm.

• **Chamomilla** is for convulsions during teething.

• **Ignatia** is for convulsions from grief and emotional turmoil.

CRADLE CAP

This condition occurs due to overactive oil glands on the scalp. If the scalp is not thoroughly clean, then the oil will build up and create yellow, thick, oily patches.

• **Sulphur** is the remedy for scruffy, oily skin and scalp conditions. This child is especially hot and hot-tempered.

• **Thuja** is for toxic skin conditions in a cooler, calmer child.

CROUP

This condition sometimes occurs as a result of a cold. A particular virus called *Parainfluenza* infects the larynx and trachea, causing inflammation and swelling. The child has trouble breathing in and has a barking cough. There may also be wheezing and rattling in the chest. The child may panic easily because of the inability to get a good breath. Basic first aid measures include good humidification of the child's room and having them sit up and lean forward to get better airway opening. A night in the croup tent at the local hospital is sometimes necessary. Do not let your child suffer too long before deciding on this route. The following remedies are to be used while making this decision.

• **Aconite** is given for the sudden onset of croup, usually during the middle of the night, that is still in the larynx and trachea. There may have been exposure to a dry cold wind during the previous day. The child experiences a dry, barking cough after every expiration and chokes and gags. At first the inspirations are not as constricted. There is dryness of the skin and a high fever. Anxiety makes the situation even worse.

• **Belladonna** is for the child with a red, flushed, feverish face and eyes. The attacks of cough are mostly single explosive barks with pain and constriction in the larynx causing great hoarseness. The child's hand automatically goes to the larynx to try to relieve the discomfort. There is painful dryness of the larynx but refusal of liquids.

• **Hepar sulph** is used for symptoms of the croup that come on due to a dry cold wind. There is a choking cough and rattling in the chest which is worse early in the morning. The best position is sitting up with the head leaning back into a pillow. The cough gets worse on lying down and any exertion causes a sweat to break out. A keynote sign is the feeling of a fish bone stuck in the throat causing great pain.

• **Kali bich** is for the keynote sign of tough, stringy mucus which is difficult to spit up. This remedy works best for blond, obese children with a gradual onset of illness and worsening around three in the morning. The child sits up with head bent back in great distress.

• **Phosphorus** is for tall, thin, high-strung children. The child is hoarse and even unable to talk and the cough, although full and deep may be soundless. Talking and coughing are painful and there is a feeling that eating might relieve the symptoms.

• **Spongia tosta** is suited for the fair-skinned child who has a dry cough with no mucus. There is a characteristic cough that sounds like a saw laboring through wood. The symptoms don't go into the lungs; they are worse on lying down and before midnight, and the child fears choking to death. There is some relief from warm drink or food.

Diaper Rash

The best advice is to leave the diaper off for longer periods; vitamin E ointment or zinc ointment are very good topical remedies. Do not use talc or cornstarch, which can cause allergic reactions. Some diaper rash may be due to an overgrowth of candida or yeast. The yeast live in the bowel and vagina and when the baby passes through the birth canal, she can get a mouthful of yeast and become overgrown with this organism. If the baby has also had antibiotics early in life this can contribute to the overgrowth. The treatment for candidiasis in babies is often to treat the breast-feeding mother and give the baby acidophilus powder and use antifungal ointments on the local irritation.

• **Sulphur** is one of the best treatments for diaper rash. It treats a very red, irritated and angry rash with cracked and even dirty looking skin. The child is hot and irritable as well.

• **Thuja** is the other homeopathic remedy suited to treat skin conditions. This child is cooler and calmer than the child requiring sulphur.

Diarrhea

Diarrhea is defined as more than four very loose, odorous, runny stools a day. Stop milk and dairy products and use water feedings for 24 hours. Make sure enough water is given to prevent dehydration. Then try normal feeding. If your baby is already drinking juices, mix apple juice with ¼ teaspoon carob powder in four ounces of water.

Homeopathic remedies for diarrhea are as follows:

• **Arsenicum** is for severe diarrhea that burns and scalds the skin. The bowel movements are frequent, loose and watery. The stool color ranges from pale brown to green. The child is completely incapacitated and is anxious and thirsty but drinks only sips. The cause can be from cold food or drink. The symptoms are worse after midnight.

- **Chamomilla** is for the diarrhea of teething. This remedy is indicated for irritability, restlessness and changeability. The diarrhea is much like that for which arsenicum is given—watery, greenish, foul smelling and slimy. The sick chamomilla child however has a red 'slapped cheek' appearance on one cheek while the other cheek is pale and cold.

- **China** is for diarrhea that is worse with fruit, causing pale, white and slimy stools. This is probably due to yeast overgrowth after antibiotics. This diarrhea is also worse at night.

- **Gelsemium** is for diarrhea from anticipation, excitement and fear. Stools are yellow-green, frequent and copious and the tongue is usually white.

- **Phosphorus** is for painless, exhausting diarrhea filled with mucus.

- **Podophyllum** is the most frequently used remedy for diarrhea. It is used for all types of diarrhea and is especially good for infants and children. This type of diarrhea is worse in the morning and is watery and foul with undigested food. It occurs after eating and during teething. The child has hot red cheeks while in the bath.

- **Pulsatilla** is for diarrhea that is worse from fats and starch. The diarrhea is changeable like the keynote of the remedy. One bowel movement may be watery and the other more formed. The child is weeping and clinging.

- **Sulphur** is for offensive diarrhea with early morning stool which contains undigested food and is burning and irritating to the anus.

- **Veretrum album** is for painful diarrhea which is watery and frequent. The child is exhausted after each movement.

EARACHES

Earaches can be a very frightening condition, especially to children, because the pain can be intense. Because ear infections can be so dramatic and people are afraid of ear drum damage they are often treated with antibiotics. Ear infections develop behind the eardrum, often from a mucus fluid buildup in which the bacteria may overgrow and begin to cause pressure and inflammation. For any ear pain or suspicion of an ear infection a doctor should be consulted.

Not all earaches are due to bacteria. Some are due to food allergies. Often avoiding milk, peanut butter and orange juice (the main culprits) can diminish or stop the infections.

A complete list of allergens to avoid includes dairy products, wheat, eggs, chocolate, citrus, corn, soy, peanuts, shellfish, sugar and yeast. What's left? Lamb, rice, squash, carrots, potatoes, chicken and appplesauce. After being on this diet for three weeks, one food may be reintroduced at a time. That one food should be eaten several times in one day along with the allowed foods. If there is an allergy it usually shows up with obvious symptoms.

Homeopathic remedies are dependent on the symptoms.

• **Belladonna** is for a red, hot, throbbing ear.

• **Chamomilla** is for an earache in a fussy irritable child. The child screams and yells, tosses and turns, and can't be held for long. She gives the parents no rest, wanting to be held one moment and screaming to be let go the next.

• **Hepar sulph** is for a splinter-like earache from the throat into the ear.

• **Bellis** is for an earache that comes on suddenly; the side of the face is red, the ear canal is red and swollen and the ear throbs. The face is hot and the fever is high.

• **Calc carb** is for chronic mild ear infections. When they get acute some of the other remedies may be needed but calc carb may be necessary to get rid of the underlying predisposition.

• **Silicea** is for later stages or recurrent infections.

• **Aconite** is for the early stages of earache.

• **Ferrum phos** is also for the early stages.

• **Hepar sulph** is for sticking pain in the ear and an aversion to touching the ear. The child gets hysterical when anyone comes near the ear. There is often pus and discharge from the ear canal.

• **Merc sol** is for severe earaches with ruptured drum and a purulent discharge. The child is screaming with the sharp stinging pain. This is the most common remedy that is required for chronic ear infections.

• **Pulsatilla** treats the emotional state of the child. The child is mild, soft, whimpery and weepy. He is worse in the evenings and wants to be held. He expresses some fear and often has a slight fever.

ECZEMA

Eczema is a chronic skin condition that can range from wet blisters to dry flakes; it is usually itchy and can occur on any surface of the body. It is most commonly associated with allergies either by contact or by ingestion and is usually aggravated by stress. One first must track down the allergic factor by avoiding and challenging certain foods. One might also investigate and treat candidiasis, which can cause or aggravate any skin condition. Once the offending substance is removed, then the skin should normalize, but this may take time.

There are many homeopathic remedies to help speed up this process, such as:

• **Sulphur** for burning, red, itchy, unhealthy looking skin.

• **Graphites** for oozy, crusty types.

• **Petroleum** for dry, cracked, rough skin.

• **Mezeurum** for painful, small bumpy eczema not on the face.

However, these remedies should be properly studied and researched before using. If they do not work after a short time, a homeopath or naturopath should be consulted. Often if cortisones have been used for a long time, the skin may go through an aggravation or worsening before getting better.

EYE STRAIN

This condition is due to tiredness and overuse of the eyes leading to red, dry, scratchy and inflamed eyes. The child may be reading or looking at pictures in poor light or may need corrective eye exercises or glasses.

• **Natrum mur** can be used for weak eye muscles. The child may say that the upper eyelid feels stiff when blinking. The vision is affected and the letters, when reading, are all in a blur. This remedy strengthens the eye muscles.

• **Ruta grav** is the best remedy for irritation of the eye from overuse.

EYELID INFECTION
This condition, also called blepharitis, is usually due to irritation of the roots of the eyelashes in infants or children who rub their eyes and cause infection.

• **Apis** is for an acute condition with redness, burning, stinging and swelling of the eyelids.

• **Belladonna** is best used for the acute stage of blepharitis with dry, red, hot eyes and dilated pupils.

• **Hepar sulph** is used for eyelids which get stuck together during sleep with much pain.

• **Merc sol** treats blepharitis with a lot of discharge.

FEVER
Fever in an infant is often quite frightening. A baby's temperature can rise very rapidly. It is important to have remedies at hand to treat the fever but if nothing seems to help, call the doctor or go to a hospital emergency room for a diagnosis. Most often the fever is due to a viral infection or teething, but it can be due to an ear infection, pneumonia or meningitis. A viral infection will run its course but the others might need an antibiotic. Dehydration can set in quite rapidly with infants. Be sure that your baby is producing urine. If not, dehydration is occurring and this alone can drive up the temperature.

The following measures will help to reduce a mild fever of 99° to 102.5° (at 103° and higher consult your doctor):

• **Vitamin C** at 100 mg. per hour crushed in water or juice; buffered C powder is good to have on hand. The only possible side effect is diarrhea.

• **Yarrow** as an herb tea or in a bath. A lukewarm bath itself will help reduce the fever and aid hydration.

Ensure that the infant or child is not constipated. Do whatever makes the stool soft; a gentle enema or suppository may be necessary. You may want to consult your doctor before giving an enema.

DONT'S:
Don't use baby aspirin; babies and young children can be allergic and it is linked to Reye's syndrome.
Don't use alcohol baths.
Don't panic.

Homeopathic remedies for fever include:

• **Aconite,** to be used at the beginning of a fever. The child is afraid, restless and chilly. Often the fever comes after exposure to the cold.

• **Arsenicum** is for a fever worse after midnight. This child is better from cold applications. There is anxiety and restlessness.

• **Belladonna** is used to treat a sudden high fever. The child is red and flushed with dilated pupils.

• **Chamomilla** is for the fever associated with teething. This child is worse from being covered and worse from heat. One cheek is red and hot, the other cold and pale, unlike belladonna which is used when both cheeks are red and hot. The child wants to be held and carried and comforted constantly.

• **Ferrum phos** is for resolving fever or a mild fever. The child is fatigued and apathetic.

• **Gelsemium** is for the fever accompanying a flu with aches and pains and a heavy head and eyes.

If the temperature is 103° or higher and after trying one or two of the above therapies with no success, call your medical doctor. Remember that fever is an important tool as the body fights an infection.

FIRST AID

1. For the aches and pains of sprains, fractured bones or concussions **arnica** is given by mouth. Arnica can also be used in tincture or cream form locally for contusions, bruising or swelling. However, if the skin is broken at all, arnica is inappropriate and should not be used. **Calendula** tincture is then used and is also a good antiseptic.

2. For stabs, puncture wounds, bites, stings or splinters, oral **ledum** is used. Ledum tincture or calendula tincture can also be used locally.

3. For puncture wounds, injury to coccyx or spinal concussion, oral **hypericum** is used. Hypericum can also be used for crushed fingers or toes or any abrasion where nerve endings are irritated, such as abrasion of the palm of the hand or the knee. In these abrasions, hypericum tincture can also be used on the surface of the skin.

4. For wounds, **calendula** or **hypericum** tincture can be put in water to clean a wound and wrap a wound; they both have antiseptic as well as analgesic properties. They can also stop a local hemorrhage.

5. For hemorrhaging, **calendula** tincture can be applied directly. For dental hemorrhage, oral **phosphorus** 6 or 30 c every ten to 15 minutes will stop the bleeding. For nosebleeds, **ferrum phos** or **vipera** every 15 minutes will stop the bleeding.

FOOD POISONING

• **Arsenicum** is for nausea and vomiting caused by too much ice cream or ripe and perhaps moldy fruit.

• **Carbo veg** treats food poisoning from fish or spoiled meat.

• **Natrum mur** treats symptoms from eating too much honey.

• **Nux vomica** is for vomiting and diarrhea and pain in the stomach.

• **Pulsatilla** is to treat symptoms from fatty foods and chocolate.

• **Veretrum album** is for much nausea and vomiting, worse from motion or drinking liquids. The whole abdomen is swollen and there is strong colicky pain.

GASTROENTERITIS

This is an inflammatory condition of the digestive tract caused by bacterial infection, viral infection, food poisoning or food intolerance.

• **Arsenicum** is used to treat the nausea, vomiting and diarrhea caused by tainted food or extremely cold drinks and food. The child cannot even stand the sight of food and is greatly debilitated by the symptoms, which are worse at midnight.

• **Antimonium tart** is used mostly to treat gastroenteritis with severe vomiting. After nausea and vomiting the child is exhausted and faint. Diarrhea also occurs if the condition continues. There is thirst for frequent sips of cold water.

• **Belladonna** is used to treat a greatly distended abdomen with pressure up into the chest, causing painful breathing and even faintness and congestion in the head. The child is thirsty, restless and sleepless.

• **Bryonia** is used for abdominal pain and diarrhea that comes with sudden weather changes in spring and fall. There are severe pains, high fever and the symptoms are made worse by any movement. There are also shooting pains from the abdomen into the chest.

• **Ipecacuanha** is used to treat the child with constant nausea and vomiting of food, bile, blood and mucus. The child is pale and in severe pain. There is much swelling of the stomach, gas, colic and diarrhea. The child is not thirsty but the tongue remains clear.

• **Phosphorus** is used for cutting, burning, abdominal pain and pressure after eating. There is great thirst and an empty weakness in the whole abdominal area.

• **Veretrum album** is for profuse vomiting and nausea with great weakness after vomiting. Any movement or drinking brings on vomiting. Diarrhea alternates with vomiting and is watery, green and mixed with flakes of mucus.

HAIR LOSS
Patchy loss of hair from the scalp is called *alopecia areata*; total loss is called *alopecia totalis*. There is no known cause for this condition, but stress plays a strong role.

• **Arsenicum** is for children who have a dry scabby and scaly scalp. When the hair is touched the child cries with pain. The bald patches are near the forehead.

• **Baryta carb** is for children with baldness near the crown. The scalp is sensitive to touch.

• **Calc carb** is for children whose hair falls out when combing. The scalp is dry and sensitive with cradle cap or scaliness.

• **Phosphorus** is for children with round patches of baldness and a smooth, white scalp underneath. The hair falls out in clumps and there is lots of dandruff.

• **Staphasagria** is for children whose hair falls out in a fringe around the sides and back. There is dandruff or sores and eruptions on the scalp.

HEADACHE
Children have headaches just like adults. For the most part they are tension headaches but they can also be caused by infections.

• **Aconite** is for sudden onset of a violent headache with great fear. The head is throbbing and the skull feels like it is in a vice.

• **Arnica** is for a burning pain deep inside the head but the rest of the body is cool. There are aching pains throughout the face and head. This is the remedy to use for headache after a head injury or concussion.

• **Belladonna** is used for throbbing, bursting violent headaches that come and go quickly but may last a long time.

The eyes may feel like they are bulging and the face feels congested and red.

• **Bryonia** is used for headaches that are worse during movement. There is much eye pain and there is constipation due to dryness. This type of headache can be brought on by a cold shower.

• **Calc carb** is for a headache that feels icy cold inside and out. There is nausea which is worse with milk. The child acts dumb and confused.

• **Ferrum phos** is given to children who alternate between facial pallor and congestion. The headache worsens or is caused by fatigue.

• **Gelsemium** is best for children who have tension headaches from anticipation of an event, even a joyful one. They can have visual distortion that can be rather scary for them and they lie in bed as if paralyzed but roll their head back and forth.

• **Natrum mur** is good for the child who pushes and pushes to do her best, thereby taxing the brain. These children are over-achievers and sometimes quite serious. They crave salty food. This is the best remedy for chronic headaches which start mid-morning and last until mid-afternoon or may go on into the night. The heachaches are periodic and go away during sleep.

• **Nux vomica** is for a headache brought on by overeating and upset stomach. The headache is there on waking and occurs in lazy children who get no exercise and eat too many sweets and rich foods.

• **Phosphorus** is especially good for children who are very excitable and run around excited and yelling all day; then they are ravenously hungry and get a terrific headache. The pain is made worse with any noise, light or stress.

• **Pulsatilla** is used for children who are weepy and change-able. The head is hot and congested and they want to be carried in the open air. They may develop the headache after overeating rich food.

• **Thuja** is used for headaches that occur after having immunization. The pain is like a nail driven into the top of the head. The child tries to get relief by bending the head back.

Children can also have migraines, which tend to run in families. They can be triggered by food allergies, hypoglycemia, head injuries or, in female teenagers, hormonal shifts. Migraine headaches can also be treated homeopathically.

• **Arsenicum** is used for headaches that come at a regular interval. The head is congested but the body feels chills. The pain is burning and the child is restless and anxious. When there is movement of the head it triggers vomiting.

• **Iris versicolor** treats the child with visual distortion, vomiting and periodic headache. The onset is often due to gastric upset.

• **Lachesis** is best used for headaches which are worse on the left side of the head. There is violent pain which comes in waves with vomiting and loss of vision. The onset can be after too much sun.

• **Lycopodium** is best used for headaches which are worse on the right side of the head.

• **Silicea** is for the headache that starts at the back of the neck and works its way into one eye.

HEAT EXHAUSTION

Heat exhaustion is from loss of body fluids through sweating and the lack of replacement of this fluid. Salt can be lost through the skin—it's not just water that comes through. In a young infant or child this poses a real danger if fluids are not replaced and adequate cover is not supplied.

The way to check for dehydration is to make sure the child is urinating sufficient amounts. When heat exhaustion is on its way to heatstroke, there can be headache, neck pain, dizziness, nausea and disorientation. Certainly, if heatstroke is suspected, the best place to be is in the hospital. Otherwise, a cool, dark room with air-conditioning or fans is sufficient, and cool water can be applied with a spray bottle or cool towels, which is better than total immersion.

Water is the best fluid to take in, and the next best is

water with lemon squeezed in with a bit of honey. This provides the sodium and sugar. Then vegetable juices or vegetable broth are recommended.

The homeopathic remedies for heatstroke are:

• **Aconite** is for fever and confusion and dullness.

• **Belladonna** is for heatstroke causing a throbbing headache with hot dry skin, no sweating and dilated pupils.

• **Cuprum met** treats children who sweat copiously, lose too much salt and get cramps, both stomach and legs.

• **Gelsemium** is for heatstroke causing giddiness.

• **Glonoine** treats a severe headache with a flushed face and copious sweating.

HERNIA

An inguinal hernia in the groin is the most common hernia in both males and females and often occurs in children. In boys there can be a protrusion into the scrotum.

• **Calc carb** is the first remedy to use and shows great effectiveness.

• **Aurum met** is for inguinal hernia with cramping pain in children if calcarea carbonica fails to work.

• **Belladonna** is for a strangulated hernia with pain and inflammation.

• **Silicea** is used in thin, undernourished children.

• **Thuja** is used for congenital hernia that an infant is born with.

HICCOUGHS

• **Arsenicum** treats hiccoughs that arise after drinking cold liquids.

• **Ignatia** is for hiccoughs caused by the emotions of shock and grief that come on after crying and sobbing to the point of hysteria.

• **Mag phos** is for gagging and hiccoughing all day and night but desiring cold liquids.

• **Natrum mur** is for hiccoughs that are severe and may be acute or chronic.

• **Nux vomica** is for hiccoughs from indigestion that may lead to vomiting and diarrhea.

• **Pulsatilla** is for hiccoughs that come after cold liquids.

• **Veretrum album** is for hiccoughs after hot drinks.

• **Vertrum viride** is for continual painful hiccoughs that are like spasms.

HIVES

• **Apis** is for burning, stinging hives, especially occurring on the face and affecting the lips or eyelids.

• **Lycopodium** can be used for chronic hives which are worse in the late afternoon and early evening.

• **Natrum mur** treats hives that occur after a vigorous workout.

• **Rhus tox** treats hives with blisters or vesicles which burn and itch.

• **Urtica urens** is for hives on the extremities.

HOARSENESS
Laryngitis is inflammation of the larynx or voice box in the throat and it can produce hoarseness and loss of the voice. It usually does not last long and is often part of a sore throat or cold. There may or may not be pain associated with it and there may or may not be a cough. It can also occur from overuse such as after too much screaming at a sports event.

• **Aconite** is used at the first signs of laryngitis from a cold with burning and tightness of the throat which is caused by dry, cold weather and with a dry and raspy cough. The symptoms are worse after midnight.

• **Belladonna** is for a hoarse throat as if a lump is stuck there; at the same time it may be painless. The speech is either absent or high pitched and whiny.

• **Causticum** is for hoarseness and loss of voice when the throat is very painful and raw, burning and sensitive to the touch.

* **Ferrum phos** is used in the first stages where there is a dry cough.

• **Hepar sulph** is for the loss of voice and cough that occurs after exposure to dry, cold air.

• **Phosphorus** is for an overused voice which finally gives out. There is pain in the throat and a tremendous tickling when trying to speak.

• **Spongia tosta** is for a dry, burning, tight throat with the feeling of a lump in the throat. There is a dry cough which is worse with excitement.

IMMUNIZATION SIDE EFFECTS
For acute reactions:

• **Apis** is for hyperallergic histamine reactions with swelling either at the site or hot dry hives and welts over the body. The symptoms are better with cold compresses.

• **Belladonna** is for hot, red, throbbing swelling with a high fever and a whole body reaction.

• **Hepar sulph** is for failure to heal at the injection site. There may be pus and hypersensitivity to touch.

• **Hypericum** is for sharp, shooting pains at the injection site. The site may be infected with red streaks beginning to go up the arm.

• **Latyrus sat** is for paralysis after a polio vaccine.

- **Ledum** is for bruising at the injection site.

- **Pulsatilla** is for weeping and sobbing after immunization, especially for measles, mumps and rubella.

- **Silicea** is for children who after vaccination have less energy, they sleep a lot, are tired, weak and have head sweats. They are unable to play and keep up with their peers.

For chronic reactions, when a child has not been well since immunization:

- **Calc carb** is for colds and flus ever since immunizations. There is no resistance to infection.

- **Pulsatilla** is for helplessness, clinging behavior and colds ever since immunization.

- **Silicea** is for children with very low energy, very sleepy and with lowered resistance to colds since immunization.

- **Thuja** is for symptoms after smallpox vaccination.

IMPETIGO

Impetigo is an infection of the skin causing raised, pus-filled vesicles. It is caused by bacteria, usually *streptococcus* and sometimes *staphylococcus*. There is a characteristic thick, sticky, honey-colored discharge that quickly crusts. However, when children scratch the infection quickly spreads to other areas.

- **Antimonium crudum** is used in chronic cases of thick, yellow crusting of lesions around the face. Washing and bathing make the condition worse.

- **Arsenicum** is used in cases of eruptions with dark, offensive pus with much pain and irritation.

- **Calc carb** is used for infection that comes with teething and forms dry crusts.

- **Graphites** is for lesions that discharge and spread around the mouth and nose.

• **Hepar sulph** is used for ulcerating, discharging lesions that are very tender and smell.

• **Lycopodium** treats itching eruptions on the face and head which are oozing and smelly.

• **Sulphur** is a remedy for skin lesions that treats infection with thick, yellow scabs and much discharge.

• **Thuja** is for the child with eruptions all over the body with itching and shooting pains that are worse at night.

INJURY

Arnica is for bruising, aches and shock from any injury, break or blow to soft tissue or the musculoskeletal system, from minor trauma to shock and coma. Arnica can also treat emotional instability since the injury.

• **Hypericum** is for sharp pain due to nerve injury in the neck, spine, tailbone, fingertips, etc. The injury could be a whiplash, a fall on the tailbone, or anything that causes sharp, shooting pains. The wound could also be a puncture wound, even a spinal tap.

• **Rhus tox** is for stiffness due to sprains and injury to joints. It may be the result of overexertion.

LAZY EYE

This condition affects the muscles that hold the eye. There may be a weakness of one of the muscles causing the eye to deviate from a normal position. Eye exercises prescribed by an optometrist, wearing a patch on the good eye to strengthen the weaker eye or even surgery are the usual treatments. Homeopathy can be used before the decision for surgery has to be made and hopefully surgery will not be necessary.

• **Alumina** is used for weakness of the eye muscles close to the bridge of the nose. Both eyes may be weak and wander. It is used most commonly for infants during teething.

• **Calc carb** is used for the left eye turning in with the eye muscles on the outside being weak and not holding the eye in proper position. There may be headaches as the child strains trying to focus on objects.

• **Cina** is a remedy used for pinworms; if a child has had worms and his eyes start to wander, then this is the remedy of choice. The symptoms of worms are paleness, dark circles under the eyes, abdominal pain, digging in the nose and itchy bottom.

• **Cyclamen** is for the left eye turning in and can occur in children after a convulsion from a fever or after measles or worms or after a fall. There is some assault to the nervous system that can set the stage for the lazy eye.

• **Gelsemium** is used for weakness of the outer eye muscles and a lot of squinting.

• **Jaborandi** is useful for a child who is still squinting even after surgery for the lazy eye.

• **Kali bich** is used for lazy eye in a child who also has night terrors.

• **Santonium** is used for lazy eye due to worms where the child has dark circles under the eyes.

• **Spigelia** is used for lazy eye with worms and an itchy bottom and chronic eyelid twitching.

• **Stramonium** is used for spasmodic twitching of the eye muscles which affects the vision. This may be due to terrors, or brain irritation such as epilepsy.

Lice

Lice are tiny but visible mites that live on the surface of the body or in clothing and cause itching and irritation. They can be on the scalp or on the skin.

• **Lycopodium** is used to treat skin lice.

• **Psorinum** is used for head lice.

Mastoiditis

Mastoiditis is a bacterial infection of the mastoid process

which is located behind the ear and consists of a porous bone that helps magnify sounds. It usually occurs when an infection from the middle ear extends into this area. There is a large red swelling behind the ear and the earlobe is pushed out of place. Mastoiditis is one of the rare complications of a severe and untreated ear infection.

• **Arsenicum** is used for the pain, fear, irritability and fever, which is worse after midnight.

• **Capsicum** is used for mastoiditis with pain, swelling and tenderness behind the ear.

• **Ferrum phos** is used for the first stage of the inflammation of an ear infection which is better with cold compresses.

• **Silicea** is used for mastoiditis where treatment with antibiotics may have been given but symptoms remain that seem hard to heal.

MEASLES

When you think about measles you imagine a red rash that begins on the face and continues over the rest of the body. However, the disease begins with symptoms of a cold: fever, runny nose, cough, conjunctivitis and fatigue. The time of onset after exposure is usually seven to 14 days and the child remains contagious for five days after the rash.

There are several remedies that are useful in measles, depending on the constitution of the child and the timing of symptoms.

• **Aconite** is used for the first stages of measles. When you use it you may think you are just treating an acute common cold and the other symptoms may be neutralized.

• **Apis** is especially useful for the high temperature and sore, irritated eyes. The symptoms that apis treats are stinging pains, feeling worse from heat, better from cold but having no thirst.

• **Belladonna** is especially useful in measles because it treats high fever, redness and restlessness. It is also good for a severe sore throat with sticking pains, for headaches and for coughing that is worse at midnight.

• **Bryonia** is the remedy for painful chest cough that is worse with movement. This condition has a lot of thirst that responds well to cold water.

• **Chamomilla** is for measles in a child with chamomilla characteristics such as clinging, irritability and demanding of constant attention. This child whines and cries for something, then immediately throws it away.

• **Gelsemium** is for an exhausted, listless child with a high temperature who can't keep warm. There is nasal discharge and nasal and upper lip redness and chapping. Gelsemium will work on the skin rash symptoms of redness and itching as well.

• **Pulsatilla** finishes the case. It is for cleaning up the last of the cold and cough symptoms and for any remaining weeping skin rash symptoms. It is also indicated for the pulsatilla-type child who is mild and gentle, cries a lot and has many fears but is consolable.

The treatment for measles may start with aconite, then proceed to belladonna and finish with bryonia or pulsatilla.

MONONUCELOSIS

This is a viral infection that causes a sore throat, fever, muscle aches, fatigue and a swollen spleen. It is called the "kissing disease" and is quite common in adolescents. If it is caught early and treated with rest, good nutrition, vitamins and homeopathy it resolves quickly. Without treatment, it may last for two to three months and in rare cases may continue as Chronic Fatigue Syndrome.

• **Arsenicum** is used to treat mono with fever, exhaustion and swollen spleen and liver. The child is restless, anxious and even fearful.

• **Baryta carb** is used to treat mono that has no fever; in fact, the child is cold, numb and completely apathetic. There are mildly swollen glands and weakness in the legs. This remedy is used in general to treat children who display mental and physical weakness.

• **Cistus canadensis** is the most appropriate remedy for the symptoms of mono. It treats the swollen lymph glands, the sore throat and the enlarged spleen.

• **Gelsemium** is also very specific and treats the mental and physical weakness due to mono; it is best used when the child becomes ill after an emotional or psychological shock.

• **Psorinum** is a powerful remedy to treat the underlying constitutional reason for the mono. It is for the very ill child who has strong-smelling body odor and sweats day and night.

MOTION SICKNESS

Children are often affected by the movement of a car, train, boat or plane and develop symptoms of nausea and vomiting.

• **Calc carb** can be used for the child who is fat, flabby and chilly and who suffers from motion sickness with nausea, vomiting and a headache.

• **Cocculus** is used for all types of motion sickness causing headaches, dizziness and nausea. The child feels very weak, wants to be left alone and tries to keep perfectly still.

• **Ipecacuanha** is used for continuous nausea which is not relieved by vomiting and is caused by any form of travel.

• **Tabacum** is for nausea and vomiting especially on a boat. The child is weak and drained of color and wants fresh air. This would also be good for nausea caused by traveling in closed quarters with people smoking.

MUMPS

This viral illness is characterized by a swelling of the salivary glands in front of and below the ears. However, the illness begins with chills, a slight fever, headache and fatigue.

• **Aconite** is used in the early stages for the symptoms of an upper respiratory illness before one even knows that mumps is the diagnosis.

• **Belladonna** is best used for those aspects of mumps that include red, hot skin and swollen glands. There is extreme sensitivity to touch around the swollen glands. Symptoms suited to belladonna treatment are worse on the right side.

• **Calc carb** is used for pale, fat children with sweaty heads.

• **Merc sol** is specific for the salivary glands and given early enough can abort the infection.

• **Pulsatilla** is for the soft, weepy and needy child. The symptoms of mumps will extend into the ears with blockage and pain. There is no thirst even with fever. It is also indicated for pain in the testicles due to mumps.

• **Rhus tox** is indicated when the child is extremely restless and has to move about constantly. The salivary glands are worse on the left side and are dark, swollen and very painful.

Nausea & Vomiting

• **Aethusa** is a specific remedy for milk allergy. The child vomits curds of milk and white frothy liquid within an hour of having the milk. There are symptoms of weakness, debility and abdominal pain.

• **Arsenicum** is useful for nausea and vomiting accompanied by diarrhea. This is usually from eating tainted food.

• **Carbo veg** is for the child who has a pain in the middle of the stomach, which is also distended. There is also much gas and burping.

• **Ignatia** is for nausea which is due to emotional stress. These children take everything very personally and get very worked up. They may complain of a lump in the throat.

• **Ipecacuanha** can help with non-stop vomiting and nausea.

• **Nux vomica** is for the child who overeats and lives to regret it. She has a headache, stomach pain and nausea. She is quite irritable and hard to live with in this state.

Nosebleed
See First Aid section, p. 00.

PAIN RELIEF

• **Arnica** is excellent for the pain, shock, swelling and bleeding of any injury. It can be taken immediately and frequently; as the pain subsides, take it less frequently.

PINWORMS

Pinworm eggs can be passed from child to child and from hand to mouth. The tiny, half inch long worms live in the intestines and at night migrate to the anus where eggs are hatched. The child scratches his bottom and the eggs get caught under the fingernails. If your child is scratching, irritable and also ravenously hungry, place some scotch tape across the anus after he is asleep and in the morning you may see tiny dots on the tape.

• **Cina** is the homeopathic remedy for this condition. It can be given three times a day for four days.

If this doesn't work check with a homeopath for a more specific remedy. If an allopathic medication becomes necessary, use it but after the condition has cleared, make a homeopathic remedy of the medication in order to eliminate its residue from your child's system (see Make Your Own Remedy, p. 00).

PNEUMONIA

Pneumonia, an infection of the lungs, is often preceded by a cold or a flu. When the infection goes into the lungs, however, there are more severe symptoms. There is a high fever, shaking chills, a productive cough, shortness of breath, headache and chest pain. For an infant, this is a medical emergency, but a remedy can be used while on the way to the doctor.

• **Aconite** is used for the first stages of pneumonia in a normally healthy child. First the child suffers shaking chills, then a fever. The skin is hot and dry with no sweating. The breathing is difficult and the child becomes restless and fearful. Then there is a painful cough and frothy sputum that may be pink.

• **Arsenicum** is used in children who are flattened by the illness; they are sweaty and thirsty and short of breath and very anxious. The sputum is dark, green and foul.

• **Bryonia** is for pneumonia after the acute stage. It is useful for the child who has pain and pressure in the chest that is made much worse by every movement. There is anxiety and thirst for lots of water.

• **Chelidonium** is for infants with pneumonia that begins as bronchitis with a deep but strained-sounding cough. The child is very red in the face and short of breath with apathy during the day but anxious at night.

• **Ferrum phos** is used for summer pneumonia in infants. There is dehydration and blood in the sputum.

• **Hepar sulph** is used for the middle stages of pneumonia brought on by cold drafts. There is lots of sputum or spitting up with a deep cough that leaves the child very weak and unable to talk.

• **Pulsatilla** can be used for the child who has pneumonia with a loose cough, great weakness and apathy.

• **Sulphur** is used for a very hot infant with rapid breathing and faintness. There seems to be great pressure on the chest which makes breathing, coughing or spitting up very difficult.

POISON IVY
The best thing to do is to know what the plant looks like and to avoid it. Once you have contacted poison ivy, every effort should be made to isolate that area of the skin and not touch, rub or press it up against any other area of the skin or clothing which can retain the resin and pass the allergic reaction along.

The treatment, optimally accomplished in the field, is to locate a jewelweed plant and rub the plant over the affected area. If you live in a poison ivy region make sure you learn how to identify both plants. At home, wash the area with warm, soapy water and never touch the blisters without washing your hands. Keep the area dry and apply calomine lotion.

• **Rhus tox** is poison ivy itself, diluted homeopathically.

When taken for the acute stage it works extremely well to antidote the problem.

RINGWORM

This is a fungal infection of the skin that takes the form of a circle and has nothing to do with worms. It is highly contagious and should be covered and treated quickly so that others will not be infected.

• **Bacillinum** is the remedy of choice; it is given once a week in the 200c potency. It is used for three weeks only to determine if it will work.

• **Apis** is used for the symptoms of itching and burning that are made better by applications of cold.

• **Sulphur** is used for children with dirty, unhealthy skin and poor digestion and irritability.

ROSEOLA

Roseola is a viral disease of childhood that is acute, short-lived, non-threatening and usually produces a high fever, then a rash on the neck and trunk and maybe the face and thighs. If the fever is very high there may be convulsions.

• **Aconite** can be given for the first signs of any illness in a child. Aconite also treats a body rash extending onto the hands.

• **Belladonna** is for a high fever and dilated pupils. It treats itchy, bright red spots over the body including face and neck.

• **Bryonia** treats a skin rash that burns, itches and stings, which is worse with any movement.

• **Merc sol** treats a raised rash with great red blotches; the skin is wet with perspiration.

• **Pulsatilla** treats an itchy measles-like rash which is worse in the heat of the bed.

RUBELLA (German Measles)

Rubella is a milder condition than measles. It usually is short lived, lasting only three or four days. The rash is more pink than red and the disease begins with fatigue, swollen neck glands and a mild cold.

• **Aconite** is the first remedy to consider for the first signs of a viral illness with fever and cold symptoms.

• **Belladonna** is for the pink-red rash, swollen glands, both cheeks flushed and dilated pupils.

• **Chamomilla** is for irritable, clinging children who demand constant attention, then reject it when given.

SCABIES

This is an infection caused by mites that burrow under the skin where they lay eggs and cause intolerable itching. Their burrows leave a visible linear trail on the skin and they prefer areas such as web spaces of the fingers, wrists, the groin, waistline and creases of the buttocks. The skin rash and symptoms are actually due to an allergic reaction to the eggs and may not occur for a week or two after the first infestation and may take a week or two to clear after treatment.

• **Arsenicum** is used for scabies tracks which are filled with pus and occur at the back of the knees, causing burning and itching which is better with hot compresses.

• **Carbo veg** is used for the child who has a total body reaction to the scabies mites which appears as a fine, dry rash all over the body with much itching. The clue is the original scabies tracks.

• **Lycopodium** is used for an infected eruption with deep scabies tracks and itching that is unbearable when covered and warm.

• **Merc sol** is used for scabies in the elbow creases and itching so bad it is impossible to sleep.

• **Psorinum** is used to prevent repeated outbreaks of solitary eruptions after the main infection has been treated.

• **Sulphur** suits scabies infection particularly well and is used in cases of scruffy, dirty skin. The child can't stop scratching, which makes everything worse.

SINUS INFECTIONS

The sinuses are small cavities in the bones of the head that prevent the skull from being too heavy. The cavities are lined with mucous membranes; these membranes can be irritated or become inflamed and swollen from inhaled or food allergies or from infections. It is important to determine what is allergy and what is infection. With the swelling of the mucous membranes, the channel between the sinus cavities and the nose can become blocked and mucus can build up in the sinuses, causing great pressure and considerable pain. The infection starts if there are bacteria trapped in the cavity that can live and grow on the mucus. Fever and heat will identify an acute infection but sometimes a chronic infection will no longer have a temperature.

• **Arsenicum** is recommended for a thin, watery and burning discharge. The area under and around the nose becomes red and excoriated. The symptoms worsen outside in the open air. The child is restless and thirsty for warm drinks and complains of being chilly.

• **Kali bich** is for more of a chronic sinusitis. There is a feeling of pressure at the base of the nose. The nasal passages are blocked and there is often postnasal drip with loss of smell and a discharge that has a foul odor. The symptoms are better with warm compresses and get worse in cold and damp. The mucus is tough and stringy.

• **Merc sol** is for severe and painful sinusitis. The discharge may be green and tinged with blood. The nostrils may be ulcerated and excoriated. The child is worse at night and worse with both hot or cold temperatures.

• **Nux vomica** is for sinusitis that includes a frontal headache. The symptoms are worse at night and outside. The child is irritable and cold and is intolerant of bright light and noise.

• **Silicea** is for crusting inside the nose leading to nosebleeds. There is also pain in the sinus cavities and a sensitivity to pressure. The constitutional type is fair and sensitive with lowered resistance to infection and slowness in healing.

SLEEP PROBLEMS

• **Aconite** is for restless sleep from fright causing a lot of thrashing about in bed.

• **Arnica** is for the child who is sleepless from being overtired; the bed may feel hard.

• **Belladonna** is for nightmares and for jerks and twitches that occur on the edge of sleep that wake up the child.

• **Phosphorus** is for a child who has frequent nightmares and a vivid imagination.

* **Sulphur** is for children who are excessively hot. They kick off the covers and leave their arms and legs uncovered.

SPRAINS

The most common type of sprain we think of is an ankle sprain; however, any group of muscles, tendons or ligaments can be strained or sprained by some applied force. A sprain can be as serious as a broken bone, so it should not be treated lightly. First, an assessment must be made to see if indeed there is a broken bone, then an examination for a torn ligament or tendon.

Massaging olive oil or castor oil from the toes up to the calf will help clear the swelling. Use ice first for 48 hours and elevate the foot and of course have the child stay off it as much as possible. Other strains or sprains can be treated similarly. Use ice first, oil to massage the area and the following homeopathic remedies.

• **Arnica** is used immediately upon injury for the acute pain.

• **Ruta grav** is especially useful after arnica for sprained tendons or ligaments or bruised bone, or for inflammation of ligaments or joints and bruises of the shin. It is also good for eye injuries.

• **Symphytum** is extremely useful for speedy healing of bone fractures.

• **Rhus tox** is the best remedy for ruptured ligaments and tendons around joints, especially wrists and ankles; it is used for stiffness after the first day of injury.

STOMACHACHE
Stomach pain in children can be due to stress, eating or allergies. Food, if it is too cold, eaten too fast or eaten when the child is under severe stress is the most common reason for stomach pain. However, if the child has had a gastroenteritis and has vomited, then the stomach can go into spasm and cause ongoing pain. If the stomach feels hard and tense then it should be gently massaged down and to the right of the ribcage until it relaxes.

• **Aconite** is for a child who has been drinking cold water and may even be vomiting. The stomach feels hard, like a stone.

• **Antimonium crudum** is for vomiting from milk. Large curds are brought up and the tongue is coated white; however the child is still hungry.

• **Lycopodium** is for stomach pain with a lot of rumbling gas and distention. There is burping and flatulence.

• **Pulsatilla** is for slow digestion due to rich food. There is a headache, burping, gas, flatulence and the repeating of food several hours after eating. Fruit makes the condition worse.

STY
This condition is an infection of the glands around the eyelids. They can be inside or outside the lid and cause pain, inflammation and often a small abscess on the eyelid.

• **Apis** is for sties which sting and are better with cold compresses It can be used for recurrent sties.

• **Calc carb** is used for sties on the right eyelids in a child who is chilly, chubby and cheerless.

• **Chelidonium** is used in cases where there is thick yellow discharge from the eye and the eyelashes are falling out on the right lower eyelid.

• **Graphites** is used for recurrent sties on the lower lid and burning pain in the eye.

• **Hepar sulph** is used for sties that have caused the eyelids to be swollen and painful and feel bruised. They are worse from cold compresses and the eyes themselves are painful.

• **Hypericum** is used for sties of the lower, left eyelid with sharp, sticking pains.

• **Lycopodium** is used in chronic cases of infected sties, mostly on the left side and toward the nasal side.

• **Phytolacca** is used for sties that are hard, round swellings with thick, reddened eyelids and crusting around the eyelashes.

• **Pulsatilla** is used for recurrent sties that are inflamed and painful. They occur toward the nasal side and especially on the upper lid. They are better in the open air and worse in a warm room and in the evening.

• **Staphasagria** is used for sties on the left, upper eyelid, which is painful and swollen. It leaves a hard, painless nodule at the site. The eyes are also inflamed and the original cause is often from mental and physical exhaustion.

SUNBURN
For all burns including sunburn, apply cold water immediately.

• **Urtica urens** taken by mouth at frequent intervals as well as locally in a tincture will help the pain.

• **Causticum** by mouth, given frequently, and hypericum

tincture externally is used in severe cases with great pain and restlessness.

• **Cantharis** at frequent intervals is used for the most severe burns.

SURGERY
A child will benefit from a Bach Flower Remedy such as **Rescue Remedy** to approach the surgery as calmly as possible.

• **Phosphorus** is given after surgery for about three doses; this helps clear the anesthetic effects.

• **Arnica** is given every 15 to 60 minutes for pain, shock and swelling. As the pain lessens the remedy is taken less often.

• **Veretrum album** is the remedy for physical recovery from surgery, given three times per day for several days.

• Surgery can be emotionally traumatizing for a child. The remedy for this state is **Staphasagria**. This remedy is very important for children who have been catheterized. The dosage would be twice per day for a week.

TEETHING
Teething can be difficult for both the baby and the parents. A slight fever can be present as well as drooling and irritability, and anything and everything goes in the mouth. The remedies under *Colic* and *Fever* can be useful.

Crushed calcium or calcium and magnesium tablets can be rubbed on the gums or put in juice or apple sauce. This will help the teething pain and calm the nerves.

Homeopathics specifically for helping the eruption of the teeth:

• **Chamomilla** is used for irritability and crying; the child wants to be picked up and held all the time. This is the most commonly used teething remedy.

• **Aconite** is used for a very distressed infant who is chewing on her fingers, crying and fretting constantly. Sleep is disturbed with violent starts. There may be convulsions.

• **Belladonna** is for convulsions due to teething with dilated pupils. The baby startles on waking and seems to be in pain.

• **Borax** is for teething accompanied by tiny ulcers in the mouth.

• **Calc carb** is used for late teething. The child often has diarrhea with green stools. The child is fair, fat and flabby with much head sweating and pale gums.

• **Calc phos** is for slow teething; the child is thin to the point of emaciation and has anemia and fatigue. The teeth are unhealthy and decay quickly.

• **Merc sol** is for excess salivation during teething coming from sore gums. The bowels are upset and there is green stool.

• **Silicea** is for slow teething and sensitive gums with blister formation from rubbing at them so much. The child may have worms, an incomplete stool and sour smelling sweating.

THRUSH
This very common condition of infants, due to *Candida albicans*, occurs when white patches of this fungus are found in the mouth. The baby, on passing through the mother's birth canal, can pick up Candida. The best treatment is to give the infant acidophilus and bifidus bacteria to build up its own good bacteria, which will displace the Candida.

• **Antimonium tart** is for thrush which occurs with a stomach upset and gastroenteritis. The tongue and inside of the mouth are coated white.

• **Arsenicum** is for thrush with great irritability and discomfort; there is great heat in the mouth which is better with warm drinks and worse with cold.

• **Sulphur** is for a baby with thrush who is hot all over.

• **Thuja** is for thrush that develops when the immune system is stressed after having childhood vaccinations.

TONSILLITIS
• **Barium carb** is for diminutive children with overly large tonsils.

• **Calc carb** is for fat, pale children with swollen tonsils as well as swollen cervical glands.

• **Hepar sulph** is for tonsils with yellow discharge; the symptoms are better with warm liquids.

• **Phytolacca** is for swollen glands of the neck as well as tonsils which give the whole neck a swollen appearance.

• **Sulphur** is for markedly swollen tonsils; they almost touch each other. This child is warm, whereas the Calc carb child is cold.

WARTS
• **Thuja** is the most frequently used wart remedy.

• **Calc carb** is used to treat multiple hard warts which itch and bleed.

• **Kali mur** is used for warts on the hands that can occur after vaccination.

• **Natrum mur** is for warts that occur on the palms.

WHOOPING COUGH
Whooping cough is a serious condition in an infant, who can become dehydrated very quickly. Treat this as a medical emergency and call your doctor.

• **Antimonium tart** treats the post-fever stage with a wet, rattling chest cough.

• **Belladonna** treats the acute feverish stage of the disease.

• **Drosera** can treat for symptoms that become worse after midnight.

- **Ipecacuanha** is used in cases where the coughing initiates gagging and vomiting.

- **Kali carb** is for the child that becomes exhausted after a coughing spell.

- **Spongia tosta** treats a cough that sounds like a dog barking.

HOMEOPATHIC REMEDY SOURCES

These are some of the direct sources and suppliers of homeopathic remedies in North America. Your local health food stores and pharmacies may also carry products.

Boiron
6 Campus Blvd.
Newtown Square, PA 19073
610–325–7464
1–800–258–8823

Dolisos America
3014 Rigel Avenue
Las Vegas, NV 89102
702–871–7153
1–800–365–4767

Standard Homeopathic Company
154 W. 131st Street
Los Angeles, CA 90061
213–321–4284
1–800–624–9659